AGES 6-7
Key Stage 1

Gold Stars®

Ready
for School
Big Workbook

slide   ride

PaRragon

Bath · New York · Cologne · Melbourne · Delhi
Hong Kong · Shenzhen · Singapore · Amsterdam

ISBN
9781472356710

Written by Betty Root, Monica Hughes, Peter Patilla and Paul Broadbent
Educational Consultants: Stephanie Cooper and Christine Vaughan
Illustrated by Adam Linley
Cover illustrated by Simon Abbot

This edition published by Parragon Books Ltd in 2014

Parragon Books Ltd
Chartist House
15–17 Trim Street
Bath BA1 1HA, UK
www.parragon.com

ISBN 978-1-4723-5671-0

Printed in China

Contents

English

Helping your child

⭐ The activities in this book will help your child learn about English. Pictures provide hints and clues to support their reading.

⭐ Your child will gain the confidence to: read and write independently, read and check for sense and spelling, use comprehension skills effectively, use capital letters and full stops, use dictionary skills and alphabetical order.

⭐ Your child will learn about: colour and number words, months of the year, speech marks and apostrophes, nouns, verbs and adjectives.

⭐ Set aside time to do the activities together. Do a little at a time so that your child enjoys learning.

⭐ Give lots of encouragement and praise.
Use the gold stars as rewards and incentives.

⭐ The answers are on page 124.

Contents

Number words

Colour the balloons.

1 = red   **2** = purple   **3** = yellow   **4** = blue
5 = green   **6** = red   **7** = purple   **8** = yellow
9 = blue   **10** = green

one

two

three

four

five

six

seven

eight

nine

ten

Note for parent: Your child is learning colour and number words in this activity.

Word endings

Look at the first picture in each row.
Draw a circle around two pictures in each row that
have the same ending as the first.

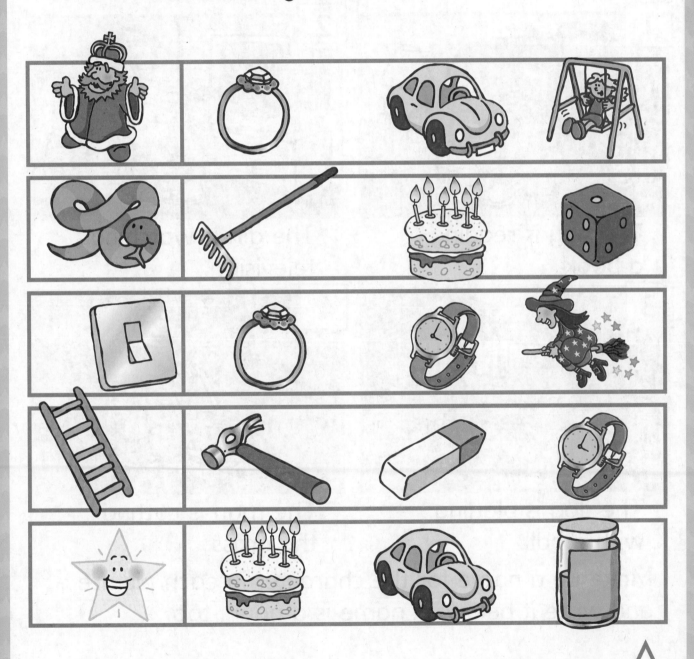

Note for parent: This activity encourages your child to listen carefully to word endings.

All about nouns

Words that name people, animals, things and places are called nouns. Read these sentences and draw a line under each noun.

The boy is reading a book.

The girl is watching television.

The dog is playing with a ball.

The man is cutting the grass.

Make up a name for the character in each picture and write it below. A name is a noun, too.

_____   _____

_____   _____

Adjectives

An adjective tells you more about someone or something.
Choose an adjective to fill in the missing words in the sentences below.

cold	windy	blue
happy	small	fresh

1. A ladybird is very _____.

2. The leaves fell off the tree because it was _____.

3. The sun was shining and the sky was _____.

4. Dad had just picked the flowers so they were _____.

5. The dog was _____ because he had a new ball.

6. It was _____ in the garden and there was ice on the pond.

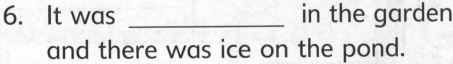

Note for parent: Describing words are important as they are useful for your child to use in stories.

9

Look at the picture. Words are missing from some of the signs and labels. Use the words in the box opposite to fill in the spaces.

Note for parent: This activity reinforces the use of nouns, capital letters and labels for your child.

Café   Shoe shop   Open   Litter
Main Street   Fish shop   Sale
Bus stop   Post box   Telephone

Dictionary

Try to write a label to go with each picture, then check your spelling in a dictionary.

Note for parent: Your child should be able to spell most or all of these words. The skill is using the dictionary.

Dictionary skills

A dictionary also tells you what words mean.
This is called a **definition**. Draw a line to join each word to the correct definition.

	boy	A creature you read about in fairy tales.
	hutch	A black-and-white bird that cannot fly.
	monster	A tool that has sharp metal teeth.
	saw	A male child.
	penguin	A pet rabbit's home.

Now draw a picture for each word.

Note for parent: Your child is learning to problem-solve as they read and choose the right sentence that makes sense with each word.

13

Using verbs

What is each animal doing? Tick your answer.

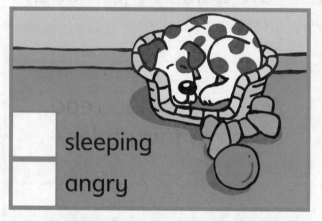

☐ sleeping
☐ angry

☐ happy
☐ licking

☐ running
☐ cold

☐ windy
☐ climbing

☐ dirty
☐ swimming

☐ flying
☐ fresh

What are you doing now? _____

Note for parent: This activity helps your child to understand verbs.

Quick quiz

Read the words.
Write the number.

two	
six	
three	
eight	
ten	
four	
seven	
nine	
one	
five	

Join each word ending to a picture.

 ce

 ake

 ing

 er

 ar

 tch

Note for parent: This is a revision of some of the learning covered so far.

15

Months of the year

Class 2 have made a chart to show when the children have their birthdays.

January	February	March	April
Harry	Brian	Alison	Mohammed
Duncan	Jamilla		
May	**June**	**July**	**August**
Ellen	Mark	Oliver	Chloe
Paul	Lisa	Kerry	Polly
Zara	Ahmed		Frank
Ben			
September	**October**	**November**	**December**
	Sophie	Amy	Brendan
	Wendy		Daniel
			Sally
			Gail

1. When is Amy's birthday? _____

2. When is Harry's birthday? _____

3. When is Sophie's birthday? _____

4. When is Oliver's birthday? _____

5. Which month has no birthday? _____

6. Which months have the most birthdays?

_____

When is your birthday? _____

Note for parent: This activity helps your child to learn the months of the year.

Fill in the gaps

Use these letter sounds to fill in the gaps: **ai** (nail) or **ea** (meat). Read the words when you have made them.

p__ch

l__f

sn__l

s__t

p__l

s__l

Now use these letters to fill the gaps: **oa** (goat) or **ou** (house).

m__se

c__t

b__t

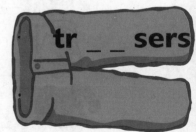

tr__sers

cl__d

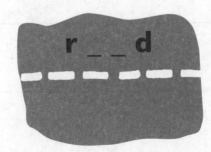

r__d

Note for parent: These sounds are not easy. Read the words in brackets to help your child.

Descriptions

Look at the picture. Write a sentence saying what everyone is doing. Try to include a noun, a verb and an adjective in your sentences.

Note for parent: This activity helps your child learn how to describe people using proper sentences.

Compound words

You make a compound word by joining two smaller words together.

 **+** **=**

horse   **shoe**   **horseshoe**

Now try to make compound words from the words below:

1   star + fish = _____

2   water + fall = _____

3   home + work = _____

4   play + time = _____

5   tooth + brush = _____

6   foot + ball = _____

7   ear + ring = _____

8   book + mark = _____

Making new words

You can make new words by changing some of the letters in a word.

Change the **p** in **park** to **m** → **mark**
Change the **p** in **park** to **sh** → **shark**

Now make other new words, just by changing the first sound.

1. Change the **b** in **bear** to **p** → _____
   to **w** → _____

2. Change the **f** in **fire** to **w** → _____
   to **h** → _____

3. Change the **j** in **jaw** to **cl** → _____
   to **str** → _____

4. Change the **br** in **brown** to **cl** → _____
   to **cr** → _____

5. Change the **fl** in **flight** to **br** → _____
   to **kn** → _____

Note for parent: This activity helps your child to understand the composition of words.

Reading for meaning

Three children have made a list of what they have in their lunch box. Read the lists and then answer the questions.

Kelly

chicken sandwich
packet of crisps
apple
chocolate cake
can of fizzy drink

Sam

bottle of water
piece of cheese
yoghurt
banana
salad roll

Anna

yoghurt
carton of fruit juice
packet of raisins
cheese sandwich
chocolate biscuit

   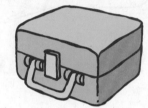

1. Who has a piece of fruit?_____

2. Who has a yoghurt?_____

3. Who has a sandwich?_____

4. Who has something made of chocolate?

_____

5. Who likes cheese?_____

6. Who has a packet of something?

_____

Make a separate list of what you would like to have in your lunch box.

Note for parent: This activity helps your child to make sense of lists and to use information to answer questions.

Speech marks

Read what each animal says.

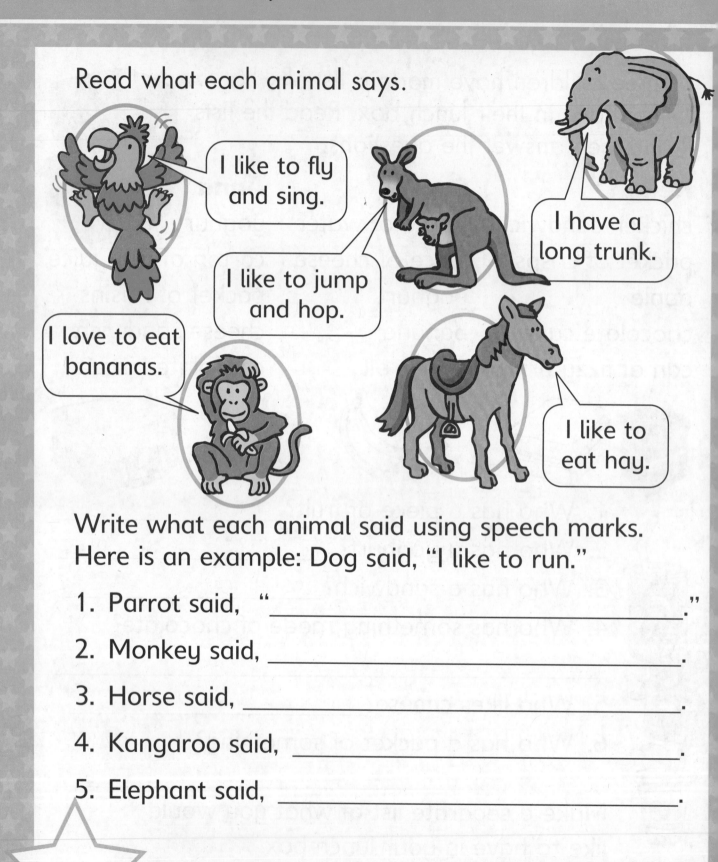

I like to fly and sing.

I like to jump and hop.

I have a long trunk.

I love to eat bananas.

I like to eat hay.

Write what each animal said using speech marks.
Here is an example: Dog said, "I like to run."

1. Parrot said, "_____."

2. Monkey said, _____.

3. Horse said, _____.

4. Kangaroo said, _____.

5. Elephant said, _____.

Missing letters

Sometimes when we talk to people we do not say every word.

I am = I'm   It is = It's

Join the words on the left side of the page to the smaller words on the right.

is not	I'd
cannot	won't
I would	isn't
I am	I'm
will not	you've
you have	can't

Write these sentences again using smaller words instead of the underlined words:

I would like to see you but I am ill. I cannot go out but I would like to see you if you have time and it is not too far for you to come.

_____

_____

_____

_____

Writing postcards

Write a postcard to a relative (for example your granny, a cousin, an uncle) telling them about your school. Plan what you want to say before you start writing.

Dear _____

Draw a picture that might be on the other side of the postcard, or cut out a picture and stick it here.

Look at what is happening in each picture.
What do you think the people are saying?
Write the words in the speech bubbles.

Note for parent: Your child is learning to select and use words to fit a small space, which make sense and that say what is happening at a moment in a story.

25

Reading instructions

Read the instructions and then draw on the pictures.

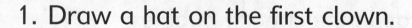

1. Draw a hat on the first clown.
2. Draw long shoes on the second clown.
3. Draw spots on the trousers of the third clown.
4. Draw a flower on the hat of the second clown.
5. Draw curly hair on the third clown.
6. Draw a smile on the face of the first clown.
7. Draw a bow-tie on the first clown and the third clown.
8. Draw buttons on the shirts of the second clown and the third clown.

Note for parent: This activity gives practice in following instructions.

Silly or sensible?

Some of these sentences are silly, and some are sensible. Read each one and then write the word **silly** or **sensible** beside it.

1. A library is a place to borrow babies. _____

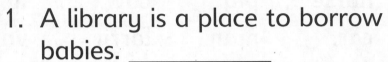

2. Clocks help us to tell the time. _____

3. All boys have black hair. _____

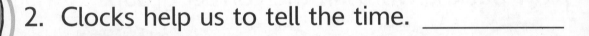

4. Teachers like to teach bananas. _____

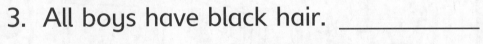

5. Cats have baby puppies. _____

6. There are lots of animals at the zoo. _____

Now write two sentences yourself:

A silly sentence: _____

_____

A sensible sentence: _____

_____

Note for parent: In this activity your child can practise responding to different sentences.

27

Odd one out

Circle one word in each row that does not belong.

1.	Monday	May	Friday	Tuesday	Sunday
2.	square	triangle	circle	shape	rectangle
3.	paint	red	orange	blue	green
4.	sheep	horse	pig	cow	lion
5.	bus	car	man	lorry	van

Now put the words in the correct group.

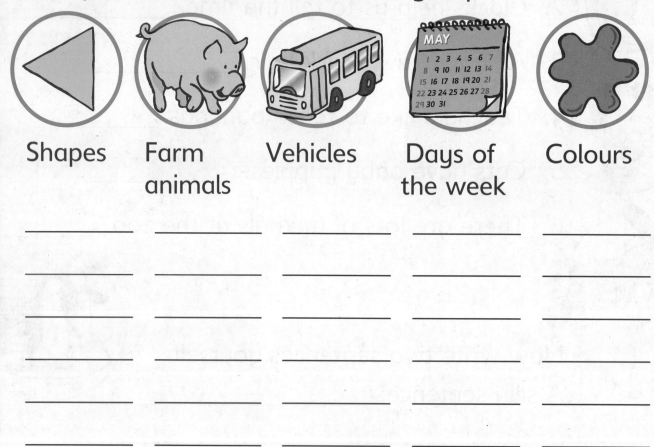

Shapes	Farm animals	Vehicles	Days of the week	Colours
_____	_____	_____	_____	_____
_____	_____	_____	_____	_____
_____	_____	_____	_____	_____
_____	_____	_____	_____	_____

Can you add two words of your own to each list?

Note for parent: This activity helps your child to understand categories of words. In the first activity ask them to explain why they think each word doesn't belong with the others.

Quick quiz

Use an apostrophe to make these words shorter.

is not   I would   cannot

_____   _____   _____

Sort these words into the three boxes below.

**dog tall grows soft mouse
run tree cold squeaks**

nouns (name words)	**verbs** (doing words)	**adjectives** (describing words)

Note for parent: This is a revision of some of the learning covered so far.

29

Opposites

An antonym is a word that has the opposite meaning to another word.

big   **small**   **happy**   **sad**

Read the words in the box.

pull	**near**	**dry**	**cold**	**full**
hard	**long**	**light**	**last**	**day**

Use the words in the box to write the antonym of each word in this list.

1. wet _____

2. soft _____

3. first _____

4. far _____

5. empty _____

6. hot _____

7. night _____

8. push _____

9. short _____

10. heavy _____

Note for parent: This activity helps your child to understand and use opposites.

Finish the sentences

Draw a line to join the beginning of each sentence to the correct ending.

1. The dog barked   into the air.

2. The horse galloped   a big web.

3. The frog jumped   on the wall.

4. The birds flew   at the burglar.

5. The spider spun   across the field.

6. The cat slept   out of the pond.

Now finish these sentences.

The dolphin jumped _____ .

The kangaroo hopped _____ .

Note for parent: This activity will help your child to use nouns, verbs and adjectives to make sentences.

Word search

Look for these words in the grid below.

nouns	verbs	adjectives
dog	runs	fast
tree	grows	tall
mouse	squeaks	soft

a	e	m	c	i	g	r	t	h	j
s	r	l	c	b	t	a	l	q	k
d	o	g	s	g	r	o	w	s	z
f	k	f	m	u	e	s	b	g	s
d	g	s	t	t	e	q	n	q	u
r	u	n	s	u	f	u	d	m	p
p	x	a	l	j	y	e	u	o	n
w	f	l	o	o	v	a	l	u	t
y	a	z	e	v	n	k	y	s	b
t	h	x	a	e	c	s	w	e	d

Now find all the letters of the alphabet and colour them red. There are 26 to find.

Note for parent: This activity helps your child to recognize nouns, verbs and adjectives.

Puzzle page

Make as many words as you can from the letters.

p	o	r
l	e	t
i	s	a
r	e	m

You can move in any direction but do not jump a square.

_____   _____

_____   _____

_____   _____

_____   _____

_____   _____

How many words did you find?

Change one letter to make a new word.

man   _____   You cook food in this.

coat   _____   You go on water in this.

robber   _____   You rub out with this.

card   _____   A horse can pull this.

fork   _____   Soldiers live in this.

wolf   _____   This is a sport.

Note for parent: These activities are quite difficult. Help your child by talking about the questions.

33

Phonics

Helping your child

⭐ The activities in this book will help your child learn about phonics. Pictures provide hints and clues to support their reading.

⭐ Your child will gain the confidence to: enjoy word puzzles, hear and identify letter sounds at the start, the middle and the end of words, choose and write letter sounds, recognize words inside other words and write words independently.

⭐ Your child will learn about: magic e words, punctuation and speech marks, alphabetical order, past tense and plurals.

⭐ Set aside time to do the activities together. Do a little at a time so that your child enjoys learning.

⭐ Give lots of encouragement and praise. Use the gold stars as rewards and incentives.

⭐ The answers are on page 125.

Contents

Word endings

Look at the first picture in each row. Draw a ring around another picture in the row that has the same ending.

chair   sock   eclair   throne

sock   clock   drum   star

ring   bell   spoon   swing

hammer   star   chair   ladder

Read the sentences and write your answers in the spaces. The pictures will help you.

This grows on your head.

_ _ _ _

You put your key into this.

_ _ _ _

He wears a crown on his head.

_ _ _ _

You put this in a post box.

_ _ _ _ _ _

Note for parent: This activity helps your child to recognize the endings air, ck, ing and er.

Learning about ar

Complete each word with the letters **ar**.
Draw a picture in each box.

 c a r

 s t _ _

 s c _ _ f

 b _ _ n

 s h _ _ k

 c _ _ d

Note for parent: This activity helps your child to make words using the ar sound.

Long vowels

Add an e to the end of each word and see how the middle sound changes. It's a magic **e**! Then draw the pictures.

cub	cub_
cap	cap_

Can you think of a word that rhymes with each of the words below? Write your answers in the spaces.

mice   _ _ _ _

cake   _ _ _ _

nose   _ _ _ _

tube   _ _ _ _

Note for parent: This activity helps your child to learn about long vowel sounds.

39

Draw a ring around the words you can make from the letters in the word **elephant**.

elephant

hat	put	tea	ant
pot	was	help	let
one	leap	net	had

Now draw a ring around the words you can make from the letters in **aeroplane**.

I spotted ☐ words.

aeroplane

or	no	on	a
plan	pan	pen	an
are	rope	near	pea

Note for parent: This is a word quiz which will help your child learn 1, 2, 3 and 4-letter words – lots are high-frequency words that will help them with writing.

Animal words

Find the names of five animals. Find the names of five insects. The pictures will help you. Remember to look across and down.

ant

bee

pig

fly

f	a	q	c	a	t
l	n	d	o	s	l
y	t	o	w	h	s
p	i	g	b	e	e
w	o	r	m	n	p
s	n	a	i	l	y

hen

worm

cat

cow

dog

snail

Look at the pictures. Write the correct word underneath each one. Then write the words in alphabetical order in the box.

**a b c d e f g h i j k l m
n o p q r s t u v w x y z**

<u>w</u> <u>e</u> <u>b</u>　　　_ _ _　　　_ _ _　　　_ _ _

_ _ _　　　_ _ _

1	
2	
3	
4	
5	
6	
7	
8	

_ _ _

Note for parent: This activity helps your child become more familiar with alphabetical order.

Choose a middle

Choose **oo** or **ee** to finish the words below.

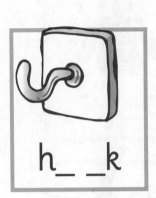
h_ _k

c_ _k

t_ _th

b_ _k

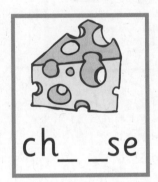
ch_ _se

tr_ _

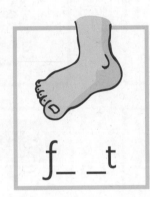
f_ _t

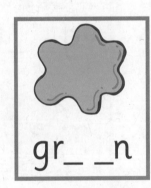
gr_ _n

Read these sentences and write a
word at the end of each.

You see this in the sky at night. _ _ _ _

You have two of these
to walk on. _ _ _ _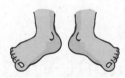

Note for parent: In this activity your child is learning about oo and ee sounds in words.

43

Choose **ai** or **oa** to write in these words.

n_ _l

b_ _t

c_ _ _t

g_ _t

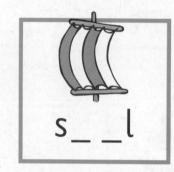

s_ _l

t_ _l

sn_ _l

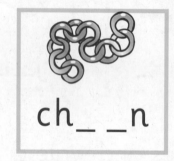

ch_ _n

Read these sentences and write
a word at the end of each.

You get wet if this falls on you. _ _ _ _

You might wash with this. _ _ _ _

Note for parent: Your child will learn to recognize and use ai and oa sounds in words.

Rhyming picture

Look at the picture. Then write the answers to the questions.

1. What rhymes with **bees**? _ _ _ _ _

2. What rhymes with **log**? _ _ _ _

3. What rhymes with **string**? _ _ _ _ _ _

4. What rhymes with **skate**? _ _ _ _

What is the boy flying? _ _ _ _

Note for parent: As well as rhyming, this activity will help your child to recognize and use magic e words, as well as words ending in ng and s.

45

Words that rhyme

Read the clues to help you work out each answer. Write a word and draw a picture.

You use this to eat ice cream. It rhymes with **moon**.	_ _ _ _ _
This is a green vegetable. It rhymes with **tea**.	_ _ _
This animal moves very slowly. It rhymes with **tail**.	_ _ _ _ _
You wear this outdoors. It rhymes with **boat**.	_ _ _ _
It swims in the sea. It rhymes with **dish**.	_ _ _ _

Note for parent: This activity involves simple reading and recognition of rhyme.

Quick quiz

Look at the first picture in each row. Draw a ring around another picture that has the same ending.

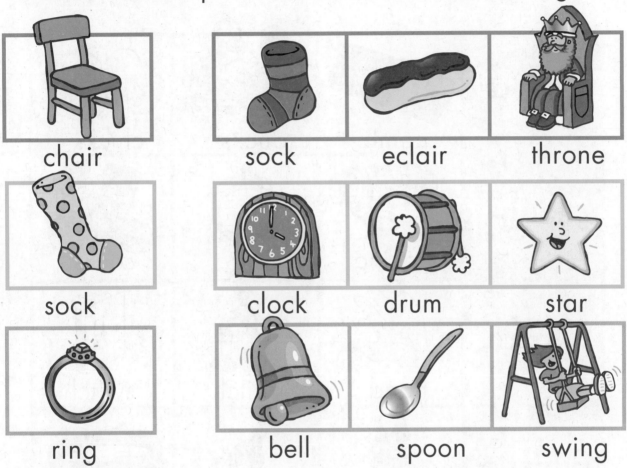

chair   sock   eclair   throne

sock   clock   drum   star

ring   bell   spoon   swing

Choose **oo** or **ee** to write in these words.

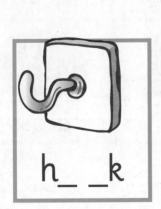      

h_ _k   c_ _k   t_ _th

Word endings

Read the word in each row. Draw a circle around two pictures that end in the same way.

bricks	comb	ducks	chicks
king	string	ring	socks
watch	hand	witch	switch
whistle	castle	bottle	belt
dress	glass	chair	grass

Note for parent: This activity helps your child to identify word endings cks, ng, ch, le and ss.

Word beginnings

Choose a beginning sound to write under each picture. Then draw a line to match the words that start the same way.

| ch | fl | sw | cr | pl | br |

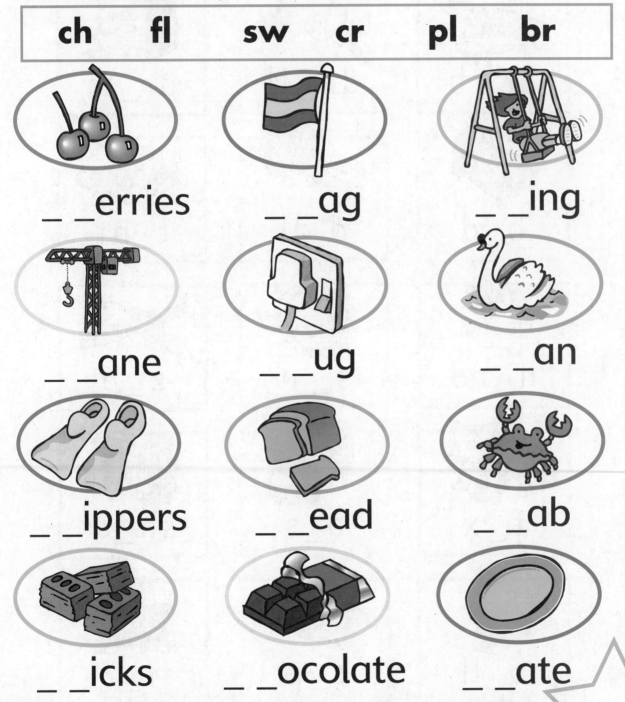

_ _erries

_ _ag

_ _ing

_ _ane

_ _ug

_ _an

_ _ippers

_ _ead

_ _ab

_ _icks

_ _ocolate

_ _ate

Note for parent: This activity gives your child practice with the beginning sounds br, ch, cr, fl, pl and sw.

Write in the missing letter **a, e, i, o** or **u.**
These letters are called vowels.

cr _ b

dr _ ll

dr _ m

b _ d

d _ ll

t _ nt

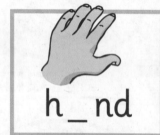
h _ nd

s _ n

z _ p

f _ x

b _ s

sh _ d

b _ ll

c _ p

fr _ g

Note for parent: This activity gives practice with short vowels.

Middle sounds

Choose a sound to write in the spaces to label each picture.

ai	or	ur	ea	ow	ou	ee	oo

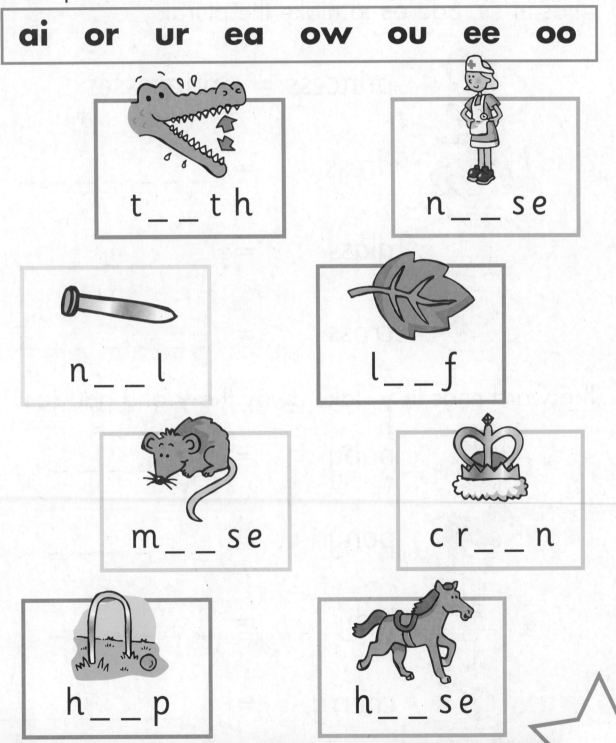

t _ _ th

n _ _ se

n _ _ l

l _ _ f

m _ _ se

cr _ _ n

h _ _ p

h _ _ se

Note for parent: This activity encourages your child to listen to double sounds in the middle of words.

Making plurals

Complete the plural words below. Remember that plural means 'more than one'. If a word ends in **ss**, add **es** to make the plural.

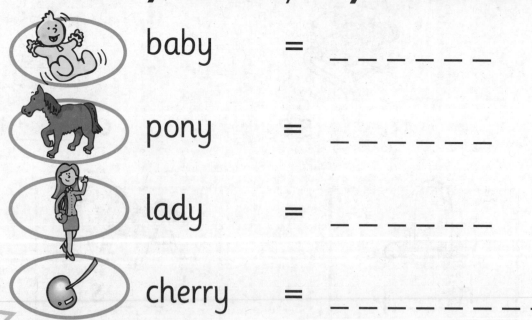

princess = princesses

dress = _ _ _ _ _ _ _

glass = _ _ _ _ _ _ _

cross = _ _ _ _ _ _ _

If a word ends in **y**, take away the **y** and add **ies**.

baby = _ _ _ _ _ _

pony = _ _ _ _ _ _

lady = _ _ _ _ _ _

cherry = _ _ _ _ _ _ _

Note for parent: This activity gives practice with the plural forms es and ies.

Making words

Make four words using the letters in each long word. You can change the order of letters. Write the new words inside the balloons and then read them.

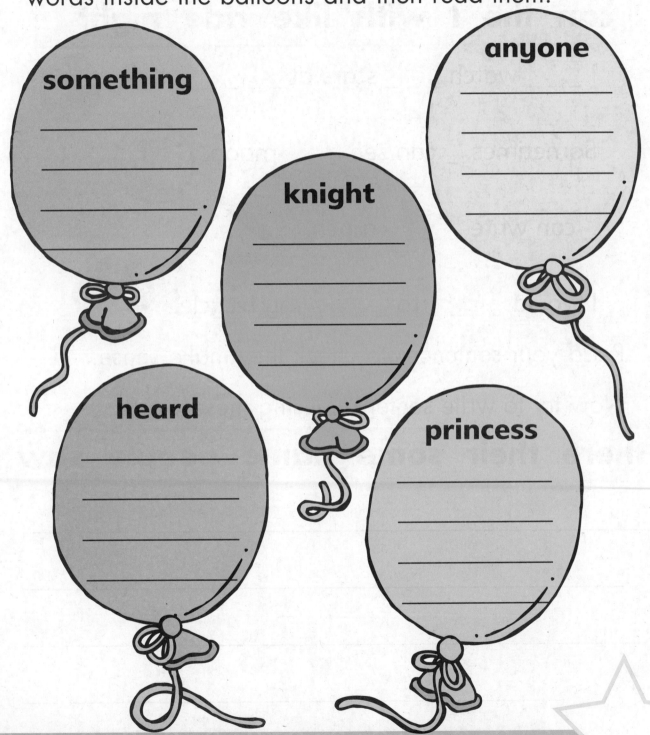

something

_____
_____
_____

anyone

_____
_____
_____

knight

_____
_____
_____

heard

_____
_____
_____

princess

_____
_____
_____

Note for parent: This activity gives your child further experience and confidence with word building.

53

Writing sentences

Choose a word to write in the space in each sentence. You can use each word more than once.

can the I with like ride night

I _ _ _ watch _ _ _ stars at _ _ _ _ _.

Sometimes, _ can see _ _ _ moon.

_ can write _ _ _ _ a pen.

I would _ _ _ _ to _ _ _ _ my bicycle.

Read your sentences to check they make sense.

Now try to write sentences using these words.

there their some name people saw

_____

_____

_____

_____

Note for parent: This activity gives your child practice in writing sentences using some high-frequency words as well as capital letters and full stops.

Making new words

Say the name of each picture. Draw a line to join two pictures to make one word. Write the new words. You can use a dictionary to help you.

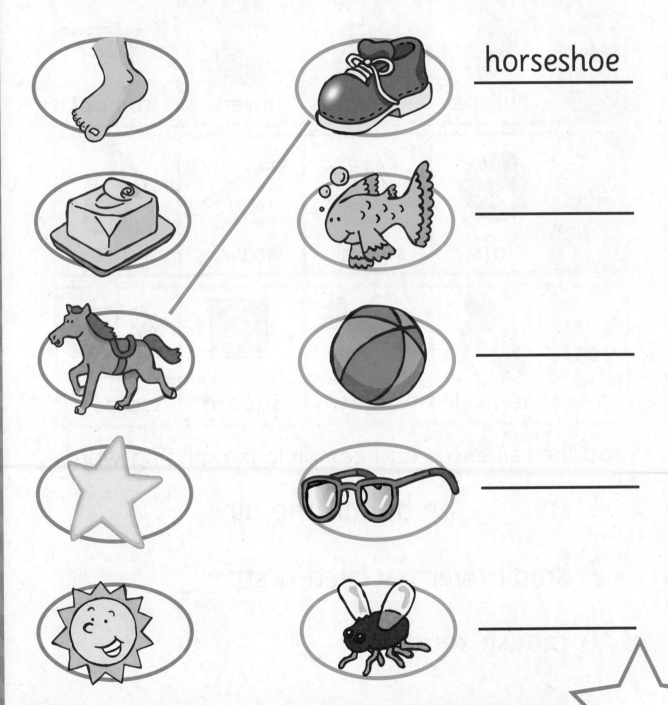

horseshoe

Note for parent: This activity helps your child to make one word from two separate words.

55

Treble sounds

Read the beginning sounds. Draw a circle around two pictures that start in the same way.

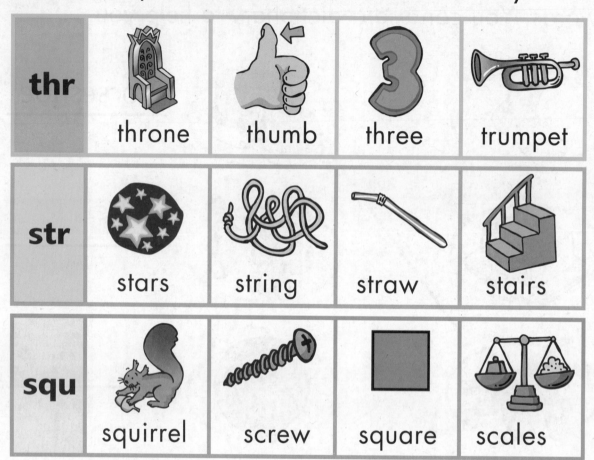

thr	throne	thumb	three	trumpet
str	stars	string	straw	stairs
squ	squirrel	screw	square	scales

Read the sentences and complete the missing words.

I thr _ _ the ball in the air.

A small river is called a str _ _ _.

A mouse squ _ _ _ _.

Note for parent: This activity gives your child practice with the beginning sounds thr, str and squ.

Opposites

Draw lines to join the opposites.

cold

sad

little

old

wet

big

happy

hot

new

dry

Note for parent: Learning opposites builds your child's vocabulary. Ask your child
if they can think of any more opposites not listed here.

Describing

Describe these characters. Use all of the words in the box and more of your own.

stripy leaping slithering brown
fast bendy strong scaly

_____

_____

_____

_____

_____

_____

_____

Word building

Join a beginning and an end to make a word.
Write the whole word and then draw a picture of it.

ch	arf	_____	
sn	air	_____	
sc	ail	_____	
dr	umpet	_____	
fl	um	_____	
tr	ower	_____	

Note for parent: This page encourages your child to associate words and pictures.

59

Quick quiz

Use **es** or **ies** to make these words in plurals below.

glass = _ _ _ _ _ _ _

dress = _ _ _ _ _ _ _

baby = _ _ _ _ _ _

pony = _ _ _ _ _ _

Draw lines to join the opposites.

cold	sad
happy	big
little	hot

Note for parent: This is a recap of some of the learning covered so far.

Dictionary practice

This is a page from a picture dictionary. Complete the missing parts. The first one has been done for you.

kennel	A kennel is a small house for a dog.
kettle	You can boil water in a kettle.
key	_____ _____
kite	A kite flies in the air. It is joined to a long piece of string.
kitten	_____ _____
knife	A knife is a sharp tool. You use a knife to cut your food.

Note for parent: As well as reading and making sense of each sentence, this activity introduces your child to dictionary skills.

Sounds the same

Find a word in the pink balloon that sounds like a word in the basket. Write the words next to each other in the basket.

made

son   tale

hare

meat   plain

flower   wood

would _____   tail _____
meet _____   maid _____
hair _____   flour _____
sun _____   plane _____

Note for parent: This activity introduces your child to words that sound the same but are spelt differently and have different meanings.

Book titles

Look carefully at the pictures on the book covers. Make up a title for each book and write it on the cover. Colour the pictures.

Note for parent: This activity encourages your child to link pictures with words.

63

Maths

Helping your child

⭐ The activities in this book will help your child to learn about maths. Pictures provide hints and clues to support your child's calculations.

⭐ Your child will gain the confidence to: add and subtract to and from two-digit numbers, identify a range of common 2D and 3D shapes, estimate and measure weights and lengths, tell the time and use the +, −, x, ÷ and = symbols.

⭐ Your child will learn about: number words, halves and quarters, block graphs, sharing and dividing, and multiplication and division tables.

⭐ Set aside time to do the activities together. Do a little at a time so that your child enjoys learning.

⭐ Give lots of encouragement and praise.
Use the gold stars as rewards and incentives.

⭐ The answers are on page 126.

Contents

Whizzy Wendy has made some numbers disappear.
Write in the missing numbers.

3 + ⭐ = 7

⭐ − 5 = 2

4 + ⭐ = 8

12 − ⭐ = 6

7 + ⭐ = 9

⭐ − 6 = 0

6 + ⭐ = 8

11 − ⭐ = 8

Write in the missing sign **+** or **-**.

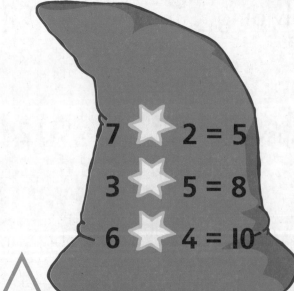

7 ⭐ 2 = 5

3 ⭐ 5 = 8

6 ⭐ 4 = 10

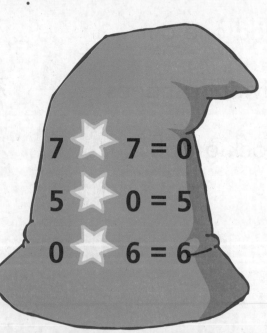

7 ⭐ 7 = 0

5 ⭐ 0 = 5

0 ⭐ 6 = 6

Join each broomstick to a magic star.
Colour red the star that has no broomstick.
Colour blue the star that has two broomsticks.

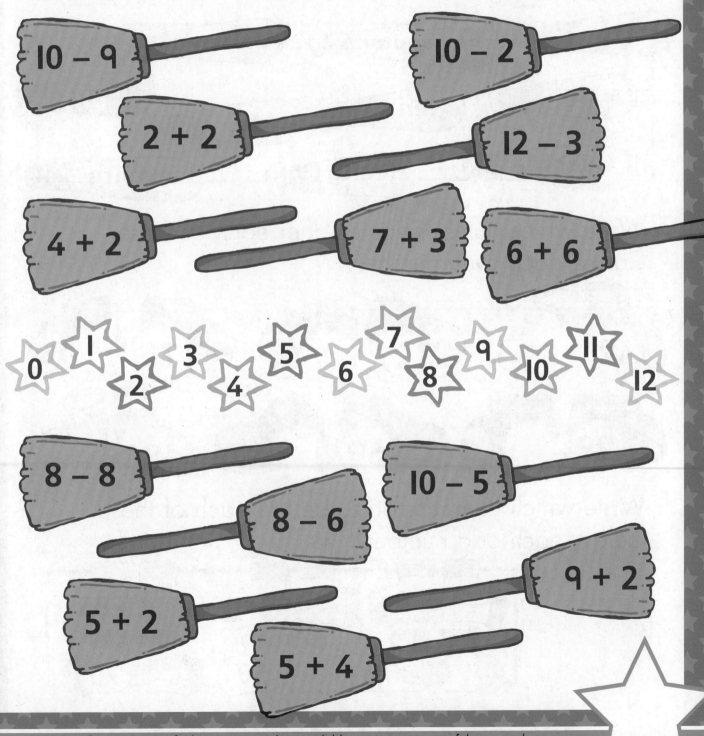

Note for parent: For further practice ask your child to write out some of the sums above on a
separate piece of paper, using the +, – and = symbols correctly.

67

Numbers to 100

Join each number to its word.

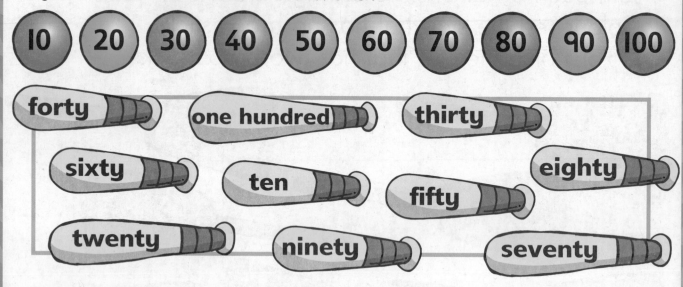

10   20   30   40   50   60   70   80   90   100

forty   one hundred   thirty

sixty   ten   fifty   eighty

twenty   ninety   seventy

Write which number comes after each of these.
Colour each even number.

42   57   76

29   59   89

Write which number comes before each of these.
Colour each odd number.

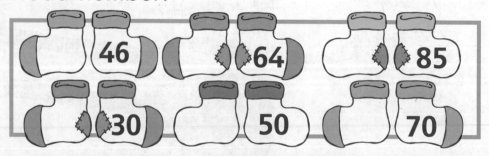

46   64   85

30   50   70

Note for parent: This activity develops your child's knowledge of numbers up to 100, including odd and even numbers.

Write in the missing numbers.

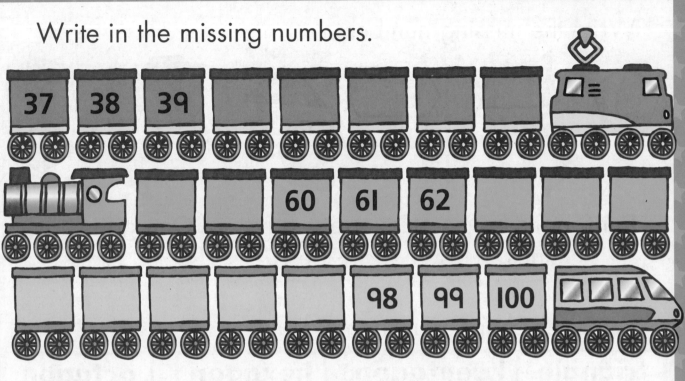

| 37 | 38 | 39 | | | | | | |

| | 60 | 61 | 62 | | | | | |

| | | | | | 98 | 99 | 100 | |

Write in the missing numbers. Colour odd numbers red, and even numbers yellow.

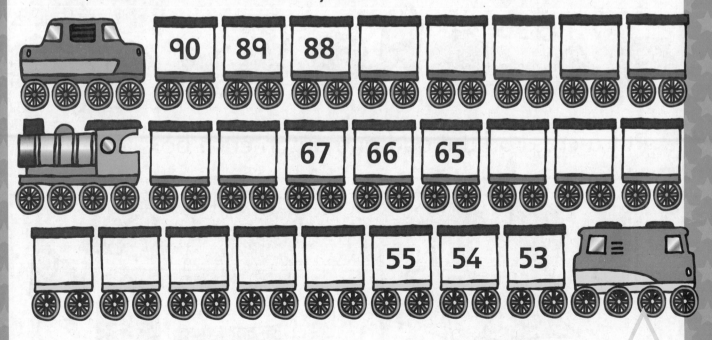

| | 90 | 89 | 88 | | | | | |

| | | 67 | 66 | 65 | | | | |

| | | | | | 55 | 54 | 53 | |

Note for parent: Practice with numbers up to 100 helps your child with adding and subtracting two-digit numbers to and from each other.

Shapes

Write the missing numbers.

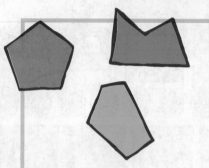

Pentagons have ☐ sides.

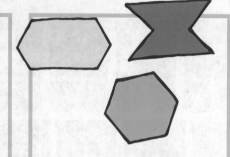

Hexagons have ☐ sides.

Octagons have ☐ sides.

Join each shape to its name.

triangle **pentagon** **hexagon** **octagon**

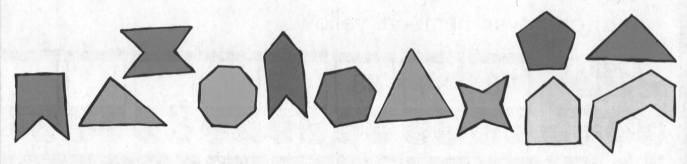

Put a cross on the odd one out in each box.

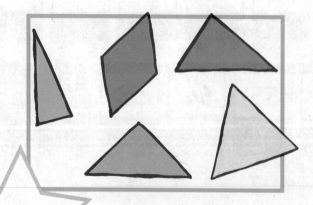

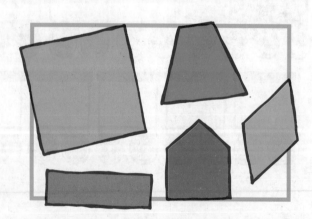

These shapes are joined to the correct names.

cube					cone
sphere				cuboid	
	pyramid		cylinder		

Join the shapes to their names.

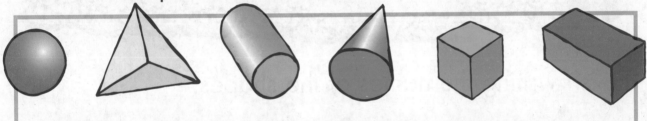

cuboid   sphere   cone   pyramid   cylinder   cube

Put a cross on the odd one out in each box.

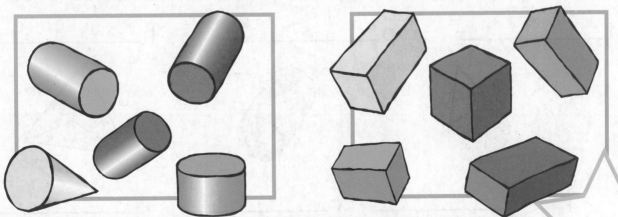

Note for parent: Talk to your child about the shapes on these pages. Point to a shape and ask how many sides, corners or faces it has. Find examples of 3D shapes in the home.

Quick quiz

Write the missing number in each star.

$6 + \bigstar = 9$

$5 + \bigstar = 10$

$8 + \bigstar = 11$

$4 + \bigstar = 12$

$\bigstar + 3 = 6$

$\bigstar + 4 = 8$

$\bigstar + 5 = 11$

$\bigstar + 9 = 12$

$6 - \bigstar = 0$

$5 - \bigstar = 1$

$8 - \bigstar = 8$

$11 - \bigstar = 3$

Colour all the odd numbers.

13   18   24   33   49   65   76   81   85   94

Finish writing the names of the shapes.

t_____

p_____

h_____

c_____

c_____

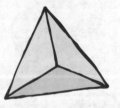

p_____

Note for parent: This page gives your child a chance to revise some of what they have practised so far.

Adding to 20

The totals on the astronauts match the spaceships. Write in the missing numbers.

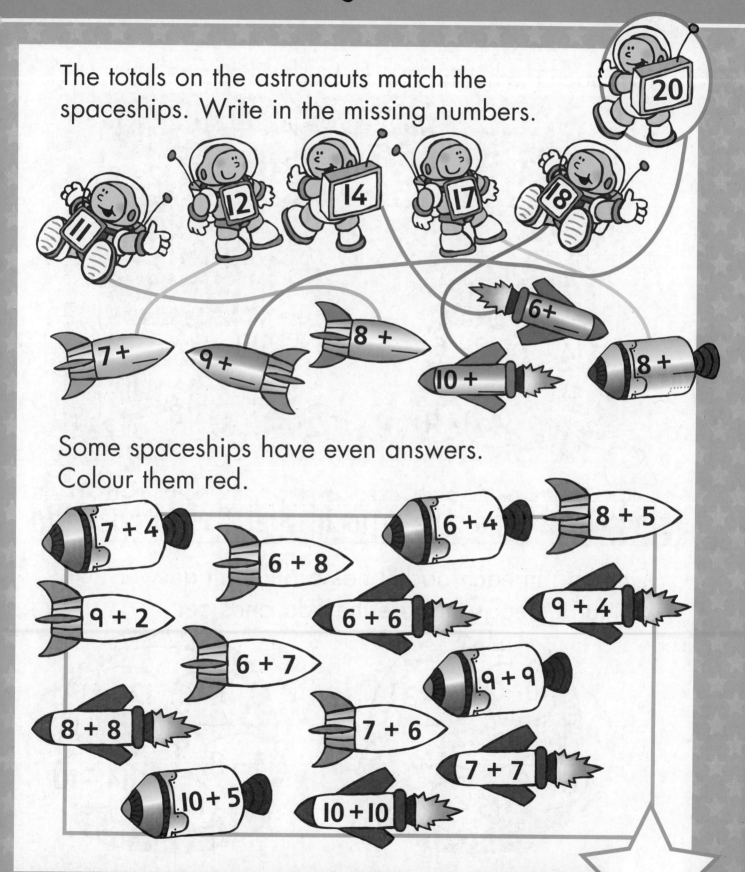

Some spaceships have even answers.
Colour them red.

Note for parent: This activity gives more practice in adding numbers up to 20.

73

Join each mother hen to a chick.

One egg in each basket has a different answer.
Colour the eggs that are the odd ones out.

Note for parent: The number line is there to support your child if he or she needs help with working out the answers in their head.

Write the missing numbers. The answers in each row must match the number on the bucket.

4   12 – ☐   15 – ☐   ☐ – 5   ☐ – 9

6   12 – ☐   15 – ☐   ☐ – 5   ☐ – 9

9   12 – ☐   15 – ☐   ☐ – 5   ☐ – 9

Subtract the smaller number from the larger one to find the difference. Write the answers in the boxes.

16 7   4 13   17 4

20 15   18 12   11 15

Mystery numbers

Write each answer in words. Discover the mystery number in the shaded squares.

0 1 2 3 4 5 6 7 8 9 10 11 12 13 14 15 16 17 18 19 20

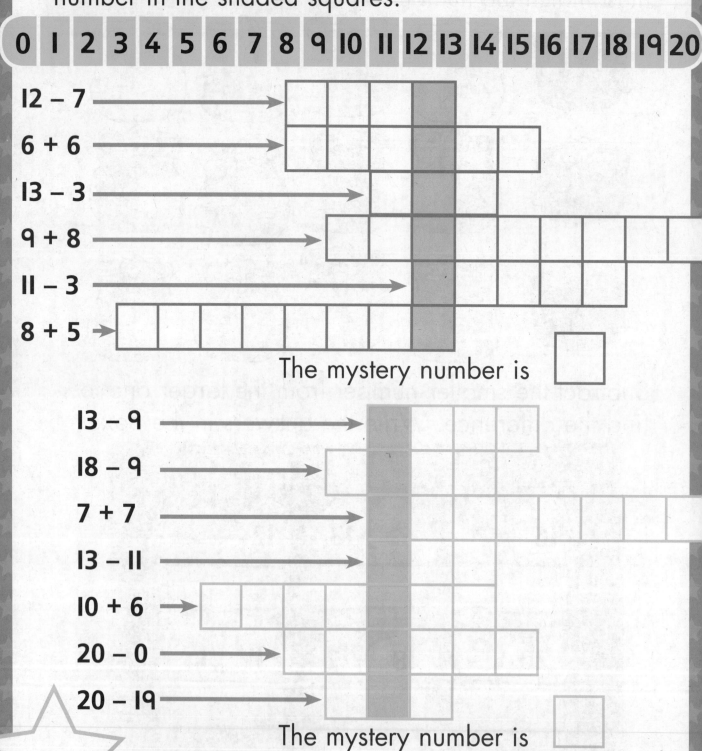

12 – 7 ⟶

6 + 6 ⟶

13 – 3 ⟶

9 + 8 ⟶

11 – 3 ⟶

8 + 5 ⟶

The mystery number is

13 – 9 ⟶

18 – 9 ⟶

7 + 7 ⟶

13 – 11 ⟶

10 + 6 ⟶

20 – 0 ⟶

20 – 19 ⟶

The mystery number is

Note for parent: This activity gives more practice with addition and with number words.

Odd one out

Work out the answers.
There is an answer in the top fish tank that is not in the bottom one. Colour this fish red.
There is an answer in the bottom fish tank that is not in the top one. Colour this fish yellow.

Note for parent: Encourage your child to write out the sums and answers on a separate piece of paper, using the +, − and = symbols to help them keep track of the solutions.

Dividing shapes

The dotted line divides the yellow square in half.
Draw a line to divide the white square in half.
Colour half the square yellow.

The dotted lines divide the red square into quarters.
Draw lines to divide the white square into quarters.
Colour one quarter of the square red. Colour three
quarters of the square blue.

Draw lines to divide the shapes into equal halves
and quarters.

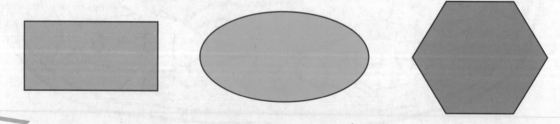

Note for parent: Ideas of pattern and symmetry are important in understanding about shape.

Block graph

Some children did a survey of their favourite colours.
They made a block graph of their results.

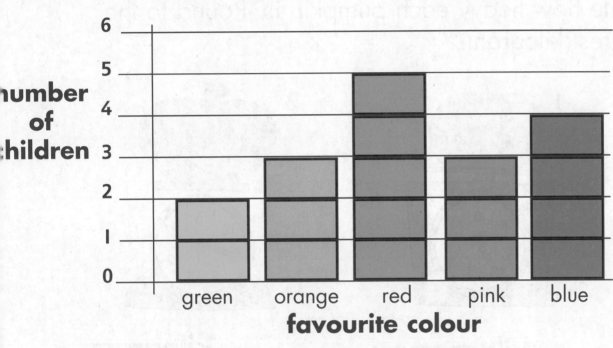

Answer these questions about the chart.

1. Which was the most popular colour? _____

2. How many children chose blue? _____

3. Which was the least popular colour? _____

4. Name two colours that were equally popular.

_____ and _____

Note for parent: This activity introduces a simple kind of graph. You can use real building blocks to make graphs like this.

Estimate which pumpkin is heaviest. ☐

Write how heavy each pumpkin is. Round to the nearest kilogram.

_____ **kilograms**

_____ **kilograms**

_____ **kilograms**

_____ **kilograms**

Note for parent: You could re-create this activity with your child using your own scales and items from around the home.

Estimate the length of each object.
Measure each object with a ruler and write the
lengths in the boxes to the nearest centimetre.

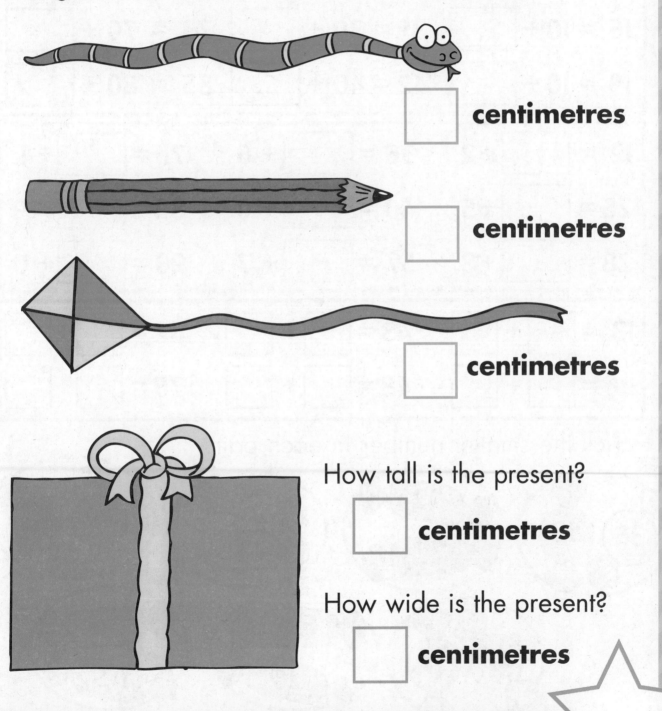

centimetres

centimetres

centimetres

How tall is the present?

centimetres

How wide is the present?

centimetres

Tens and ones

Write the missing numbers using tens and ones.

15 = 10 + ☐   31 = 30 + ☐   64 = 60 + ☐

16 = 10 + ☐   39 = 30 + ☐   73 = 70 + ☐

19 = 10 + ☐   42 = 40 + ☐   85 = 80 + ☐

12 = ☐ + 2   36 = ☐ + 6   71 = ☐ + 1

25 = ☐ + 5   40 = ☐ + 0   89 = ☐ + 9

28 = ☐ + 8   57 = ☐ + 7   90 = ☐ + 0

13 = ☐ + ☐   43 = ☐ + ☐   62 = ☐ + ☐

26 = ☐ + ☐   48 = ☐ + ☐   75 = ☐ + ☐

Tick the smaller number in each pair.

Note for parent: This page shows how large numbers are built up using tens and ones. Ask your child to explain how they decided which number was bigger in the sweets activity.

Words and numbers

Write the correct number on each child.

Add 1 to each number.

39 46 73

40

Subtract 1 from each number.

50 44 68

Add 10 to each number.

34 51 69

Subtract 10 from each number.

28 37 52

Note for parent: This activity gives further practice in working with large numbers.

Write the missing numbers on the clock face.

Make the clock show 7 o'clock.

Make each of these clocks and watches show 4 o'clock.

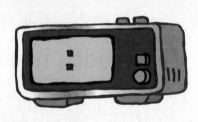

Make each of these clocks and watches show half-past 2.

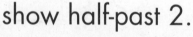

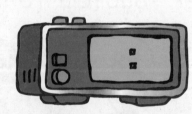

One hour passes on each clock. Write the new times.

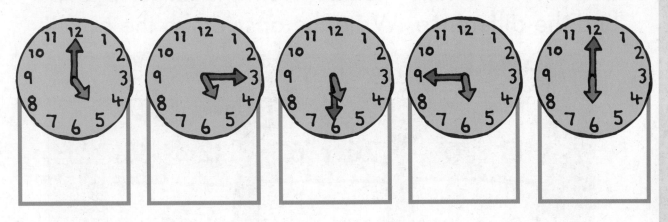

Join clocks that say the same time.

Draw in the missing minute hand on each clock.

5:45   **9:15**   **6:30**   **4:15**

Quick quiz

Subtract the smaller number from the larger one to find the difference. Write the answers in the boxes.

Colour all the sacks that have EVEN answers.

Write the missing numbers.

twenty-six = 20 + ☐   **forty-eight** = 40 + ☐

seventy-nine = 70 + ☐   **thirty-two** = ☐ + 2

sixty-five = ☐ + 5   **eighty-four** = ☐ + 4

Join the matching answers. Circle the odd one out.

30 + 5   8 + 8   10 + 6

60 + 2   10 + 10   25 + 10   50 + 12

Note for parent: Encourage your child to look back to help them revise if needed.

Twos and tens

Write the missing numbers in the twos pattern.

| 2 | 4 | 6 | | | | | | | |

Write the hidden number in each box.

☐ × 2 = 6   ☐ × 2 = 10   ☐ × 2 = 16

2 × ☐ = 20   2 × ☐ = 4   2 × ☐ = 14

☐ × 2 = 2   ☐ × 2 = 18   ☐ × 2 = 12

Write the missing numbers in the tens pattern.

| 10 | 20 | 30 | | | | | | |

Write the hidden number in each box.

☐ × 10 = 30   ☐ × 10 = 60   ☐ × 10 = 20

10 × ☐ = 40   10 × ☐ = 90   10 × ☐ = 100

☐ × 10 = 80   ☐ × 10 = 10

Note for parent: This is an early start to learning multiplication tables.

Fives, twos and tens

Write the missing numbers on the fives pattern.

5   10   15

Write the hidden number beside each leaf.

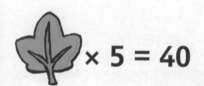 × 5 = 5

× 5 = 15

× 5 = 45

5 × = 25

5 × = 30

5 × = 10

× 5 = 40

× 5 = 20

× 5 = 35

Write how many fives are in each group.

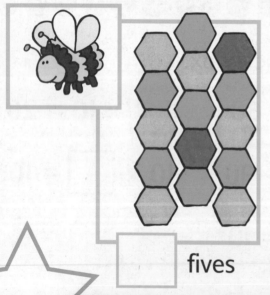

fives

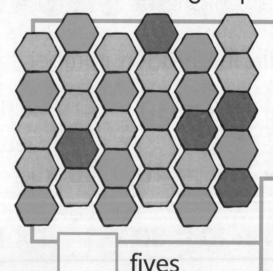

fives

Note for parent: Explain to your child that 5 + 5 + 5 is the same as 5 x 3. This is called 'repeated addition' and is a useful method in multiplication for your child to understand.

Write in the answers to these tables.

2 × 1 = ☐	5 × 1 = ☐	10 × 1 = ☐
2 × 2 = ☐	5 × 2 = ☐	10 × 2 = ☐
2 × 3 = ☐	5 × 3 = ☐	10 × 3 = ☐
2 × 4 = ☐	5 × 4 = ☐	10 × 4 = ☐
2 × 5 = ☐	5 × 5 = ☐	10 × 5 = ☐
2 × 6 = ☐	5 × 6 = ☐	10 × 6 = ☐
2 × 7 = ☐	5 × 7 = ☐	10 × 7 = ☐
2 × 8 = ☐	5 × 8 = ☐	10 × 8 = ☐
2 × 9 = ☐	5 × 9 = ☐	10 × 9 = ☐
2 × 10 = ☐	5 × 10 = ☐	10 × 10 = ☐

Work out the answers. Join each saucer to a cup.

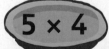  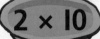 

Note for parent: Encourage your child to count in twos, fives and tens. Ask them if they can use this skill to count up to 100 objects, e.g. 100 coins or paperclips.

Sharing

Join the balls to the clowns.
Each clown must have the same number of balls.

balls for
each clown

balls for
each clown

balls for
each clown

Note for parent: This activity is an introduction to division.

Write how many twos are in each tree.

twos

twos

Write how many threes are on each pond.

threes

threes

Write how many fours are in each bag.

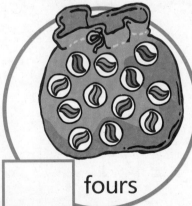

fours

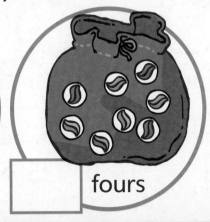

fours

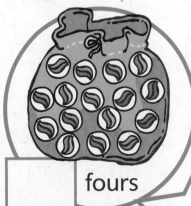

fours

Dividing

Draw lines to divide the beach items fairly.
Write the numbers in the boxes.

between 2 people

6 ÷ 2 = ☐

between 2 people

8 ÷ 2 = ☐

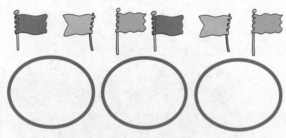

between 3 people

6 ÷ 3 = ☐

between 3 people

9 ÷ 3 = ☐

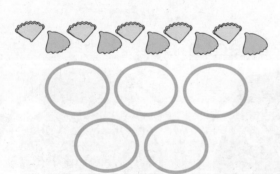

between 5 people

10 ÷ 5 = ☐

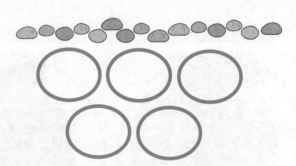

between 5 people

15 ÷ 5 = ☐

Note for parent: This page introduces your child to the ÷ symbol. For further practice your child could write out the divisions using the ÷ and = symbols.

Write in the answers to these tables.

2 ÷ 2 = ☐	5 ÷ 5 = ☐	10 ÷ 10 = ☐
4 ÷ 2 = ☐	10 ÷ 5 = ☐	20 ÷ 10 = ☐
6 ÷ 2 = ☐	15 ÷ 5 = ☐	30 ÷ 10 = ☐
8 ÷ 2 = ☐	20 ÷ 5 = ☐	40 ÷ 10 = ☐
10 ÷ 2 = ☐	25 ÷ 5 = ☐	50 ÷ 10 = ☐
12 ÷ 2 = ☐	30 ÷ 5 = ☐	60 ÷ 10 = ☐
14 ÷ 2 = ☐	35 ÷ 5 = ☐	70 ÷ 10 = ☐
16 ÷ 2 = ☐	40 ÷ 5 = ☐	80 ÷ 10 = ☐
18 ÷ 2 = ☐	45 ÷ 5 = ☐	90 ÷ 10 = ☐
20 ÷ 2 = ☐	50 ÷ 5 = ☐	100 ÷ 10 = ☐

Work out the answers. Join each saucer to a cup.

Addition and Subtraction

Helping your child

⭐ The activities in this book will help your child to learn about addition and subtraction. Pictures provide hints and clues to support your child's calculations.

⭐ Your child will gain the confidence to: add and subtract to and from two-digit numbers, use addition and subtraction bonds, use repeated addition as a method of multiplying, understand the +, −, x and = symbols and calculate the value of an unknown number within a number sentence.

⭐ Your child will learn about: doubles and halves, odd and even numbers and two- and three-digit numbers.

⭐ Set aside time to do the activities together. Do a little at a time so that your child enjoys learning.

⭐ Give lots of encouragement and praise.
Use the gold stars as rewards and incentives.

⭐ The answers are on page 127.

Contents

Counting on

Use the number line to count on. Show the jumps and write the answers. The first one has been done for you.

12 + 3 = $\boxed{15}$

10 11 12 13 14 15 16 17 18 19

8 + 4 = $\boxed{}$

6 7 8 9 10 11 12 13 14 15

7 + 7 = $\boxed{}$

7 8 9 10 11 12 13 14 15 16

Complete the sums below.

9 + 6 = $\boxed{}$ 13 + 4 = $\boxed{}$ 15 + 5 = $\boxed{}$

11 + 10 = $\boxed{}$ 16 + 13 = $\boxed{}$ 20 + 20 = $\boxed{}$

32 + 21 = $\boxed{}$ 55 + 27 = $\boxed{}$

Note for parent: Your child will be familiar with using number lines to count on. This activity recaps that knowledge and develops the mental addition skills they will be learning at this age.

Counting back

Show the jumps and write the answers.

14 − 5 = ☐

6 7 8 9 10 11 12 13 14 15 16 17

18 − 6 = ☐

9 10 11 12 13 14 15 16 17 18 19 20

16 − 7 = ☐

7 8 9 10 11 12 13 14 15 16 17 18

Complete the sums below.

10 − 4 = ☐   13 − 5 = ☐   11 − 3 = ☐

14 − 13 = ☐   19 − 11 = ☐   20 − 10 = ☐

46 − 25 = ☐   63 − 37 = ☐

Note for parent: Your child will be familiar with counting back as a method of taking away and developing mental subtraction skills at this age.

97

Making totals

Count each set. Write the totals.

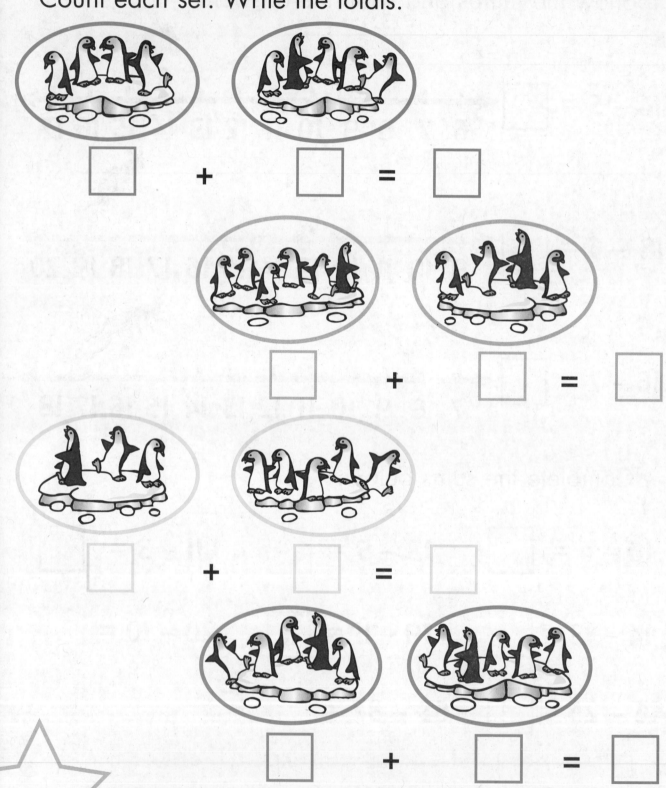

Note for parent: This activity gives your child practice in combining sets to make totals.

Draw snowflakes to make the totals.

$6 + \boxed{} = 10$

$5 + \boxed{} = 12$

$\boxed{} + 3 = 10$

Join pairs of numbers that total 12.

Taking away

Cross out four items on each shelf.
Write how many are left.

$6 - 4 =$ ☐

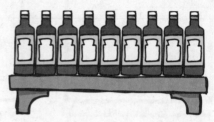

$9 - 4 =$ ☐

☐ $- 4 =$ ☐

☐ $- 4 =$ ☐

Cross out five in each set. Write how many are left.

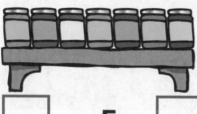

☐ $- 5 =$ ☐

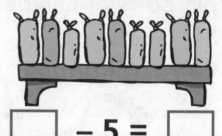

☐ $- 5 =$ ☐

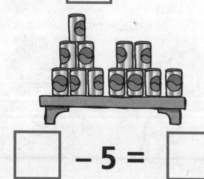

☐ $- 5 =$ ☐

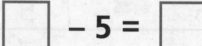

☐ $- 5 =$ ☐

Note for parent: This activity gives your child practice in subtraction by taking amounts away.

Coco the clown has 12 balloons. Write the new totals in the boxes.

Sam buys
3 balloons.

12 – 3 = ☐

Coco loses
1 balloon.

9 – 1 = ☐

Lucy buys
5 balloons.

8 – 5 = ☐

Coco gives
2 balloons away.

3 – 2 = ☐

Number machines

Total the numbers going into the machines.

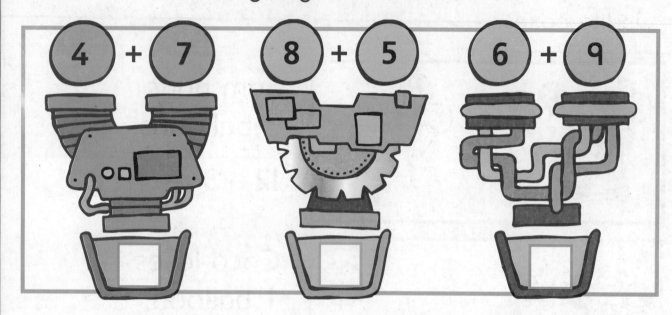

Write the numbers coming out of this machine.

Note for parent: Ask your child to look at the numbers going into each machine and work out the numbers coming out mentally, rather than counting on their fingers, for example.

Write the numbers coming out of these machines.

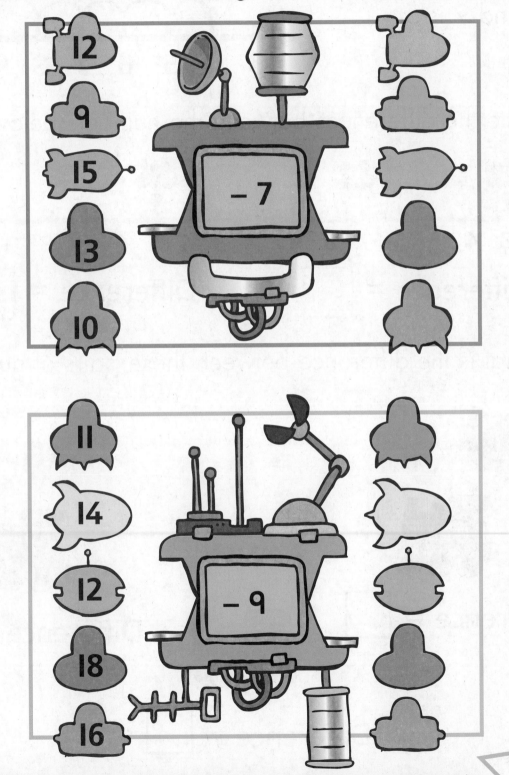

Note for parent: Ask your child to write out some of the sums from these pages on a separate piece of paper, using the +, − and = symbols.

103

The difference between
4 and 9 is 5.

Write the differences between the numbers below.

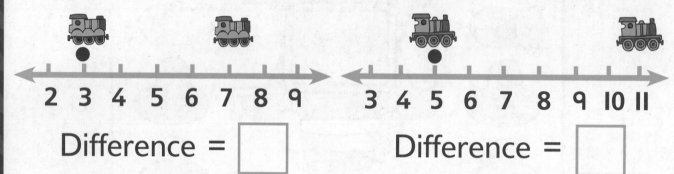

Difference = ☐   Difference = ☐

What is the difference between these pairs of numbers?

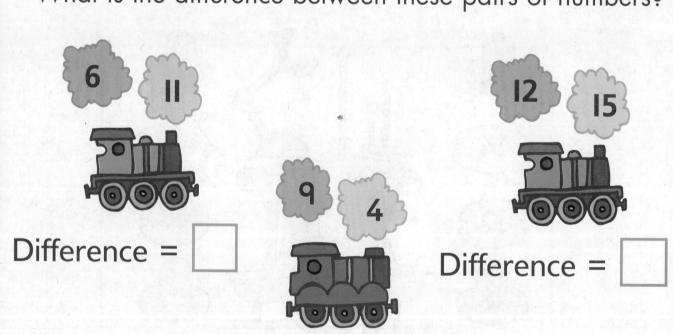

Difference = ☐

Difference = ☐

Difference = ☐

Note for parent: To find the difference between two numbers ask your child to count on from the lower number.

Find the pairs of numbers with a difference of 6.
Colour each matching pair.

Fill in the missing number so that each submarine has
a difference of 5. The first one has been done for you.

Make the totals in the middle of the spacestations in different ways. The first one has been done for you.

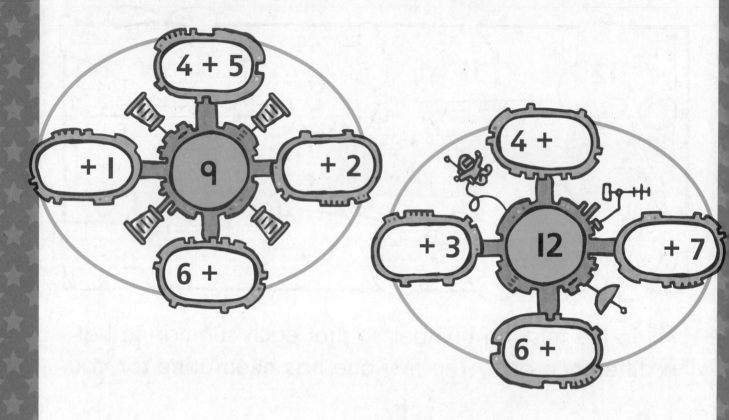

Write your own numbers for this spacestation.

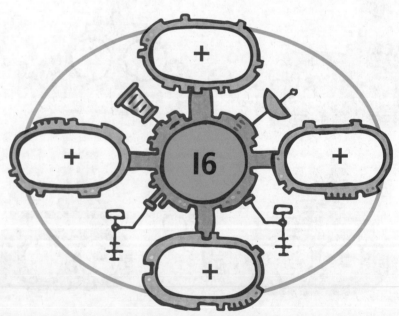

Note for parent: Addition bonds are all the different ways that a total can be made with two numbers.

Count each set. Write the total.

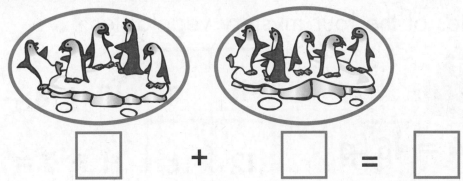

☐ + ☐ = ☐

Cross out four items on each shelf. Write how many are left.

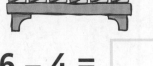

6 – 4 = ☐   ☐ – 4 = ☐

Write the numbers coming out of this machine.

Note for parent: This page is a chance to revise some of the learning so far.

107

Adding to 20

Answer each of these sums. Use the code to find the names of the four mystery vegetables.

12 + 4 = **16** p

9 + 9 = ☐ _

6 + 5 = ☐ _

7 + 5 = ☐ _

2 + 9 = ☐ _

10 + 7 = ☐ _

8 + 9 = ☐ _

9 + 6 = ☐ _

10 + 9 = ☐ _

11	a
12	c
13	i
14	n
15	o
16	p
17	r
18	e
19	t
20	b

12 + 8 = ☐ _

11 + 7 = ☐ _

8 + 3 = ☐ _

7 + 7 = ☐ _

8 + 8 = ☐ _

11 + 4 = ☐ _

12 + 7 = ☐ _

6 + 5 = ☐ _

5 + 14 = ☐ _

8 + 7 = ☐ _

Fill in the missing numbers to complete these addition walls. The first one has been done for you.

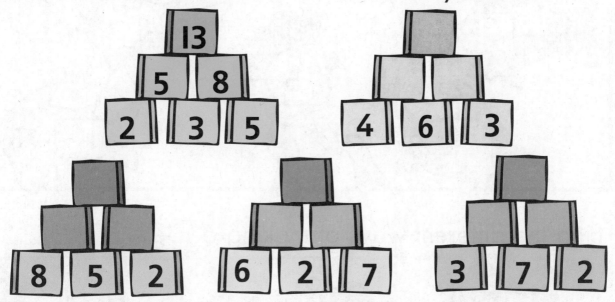

Write the numbers to complete these adding chains. The first answer has been done for you.

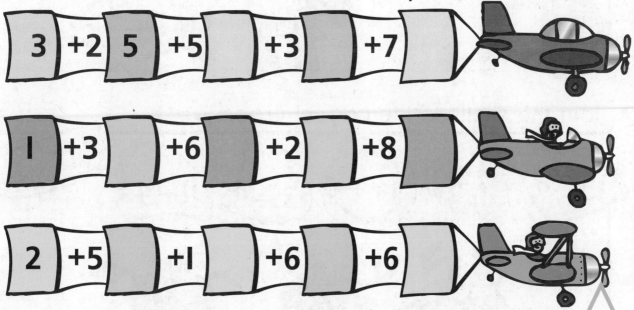

Subtraction bonds

Find the different ways of making 5.

12 − ☐   9 − ☐   ☐ − 8   5   ☐ − 6

Find the different ways of making 6.

☐ − 4   11 − ☐   9 − ☐   6   14 − ☐

Join the shells to the correct crabs.

15 − 8   17 − 9   14 − 6   13 − 9   11 − 4   12 − 8

4   7   8

Note for parent: Children generally find subtraction bonds more difficult than addition bonds.

Circle the odd one out in each set.

Join the matching answers.

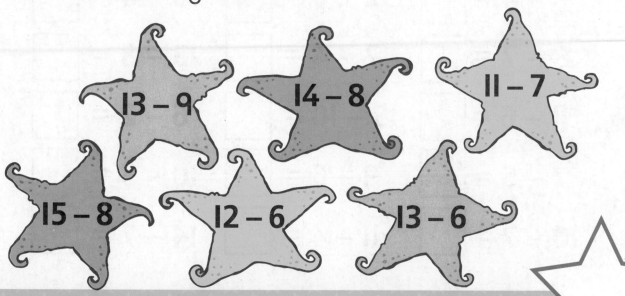

Note for parent: If your child knows that 5 + 7 = 12, then they can work out that 12 − 7 = 5.
Ask your child to write out any bonds they struggle with in this way.

Take away facts

Write the answers to these in words. Find the mystery number in the shaded squares.

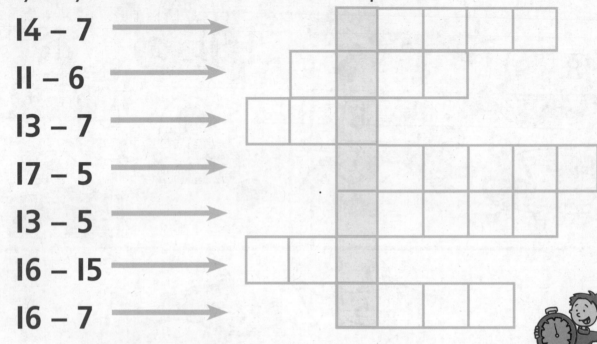

14 – 7 ⟶

11 – 6 ⟶

13 – 7 ⟶

17 – 5 ⟶

13 – 5 ⟶

16 – 15 ⟶

16 – 7 ⟶

Answer these as quickly as you can.
Time yourself and try to beat your best time.

9 – 4 = ☐   12 – 6 = ☐   8 – 4 = ☐

8 – 7 = ☐   7 – 4 = ☐   13 – 8 = ☐

11 – 6 = ☐   15 – 10 = ☐   6 – 2 = ☐

7 – 5 = ☐   9 – 6 = ☐   10 – 5 = ☐

10 – 7 = ☐   11 – 4 = ☐   14 – 7 = ☐

Note for parent: These activities give practice in learning the subtraction facts within 20.

Fill in the missing numbers to make each total.
The first one has been done for you.

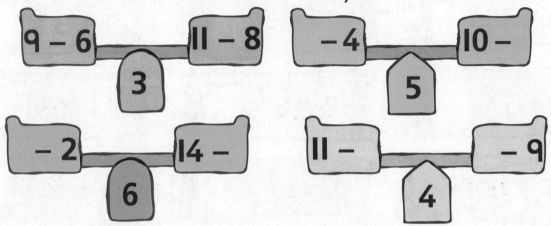

Write in your own numbers to make the total.

Complete the number trails back to zero.

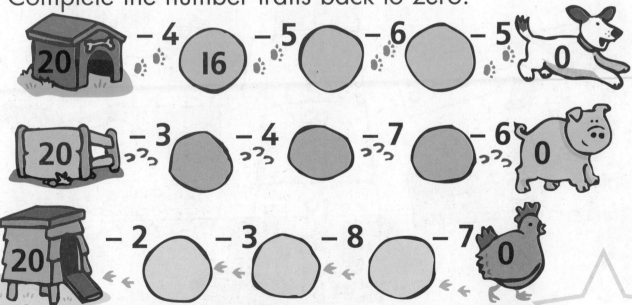

113

Doubles

Answer these doubles.

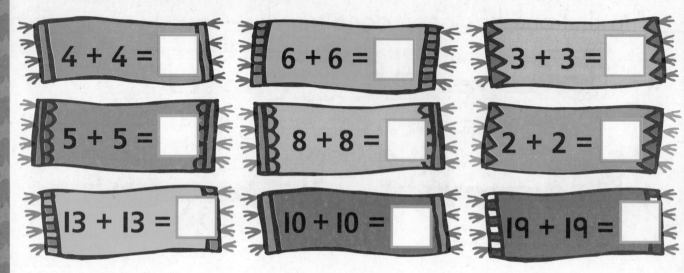

4 + 4 = ☐

6 + 6 = ☐

3 + 3 = ☐

5 + 5 = ☐

8 + 8 = ☐

2 + 2 = ☐

13 + 13 = ☐

10 + 10 = ☐

19 + 19 = ☐

Join the sums to the correct answers.

3 + 4

5 + 6

8 + 9

10 + 9

5 + 4

6 + 7

8 + 7

7
9
11
13
15
17
19

Note for parent: Ask your child if he or she can work out what half of each double is. You can also use doubles to work out 'near doubles', e.g. 6 + 6 is 12, so 6 + 7 is one more.

Add the number in the circles together 3 times.
Write the total in the centre.
The first one has been completed for you.

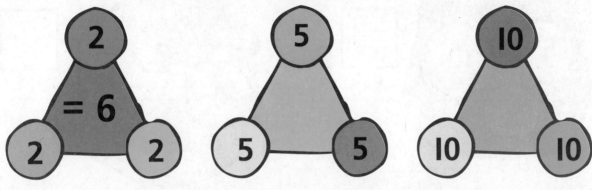

2 + 2 + 2 is the same as 2 x 3 = 6

Write the missing numbers below.

5 + 5 + ☐ = 5 x 3 = 15
10 + 10 + 10 = ☐ x 3 = ☐
2 + 2 + 2 + 2 = 2 x 4 = ☐
5 + ☐ + 5 + 5 + 5 = ☐ x 5 = 25
10 + 10 + 10 + 10 + 10 + 10 = 10 x ☐ = ☐

Note for parent: Repeated addition introduces the concept of multiplication and using the x symbol.
Ask your child to write out the calculations separately using the +, x and = symbols.

Money totals

How much money is in each purse? Write the answers in the boxes.

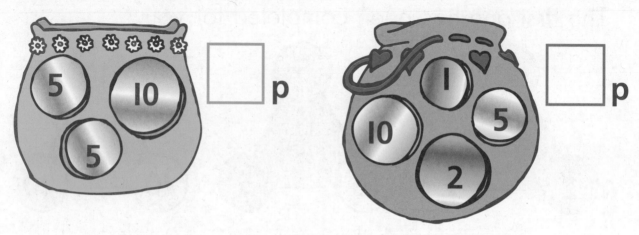

What is the total cost of each group of items? Write the answers in the boxes.

£ ☐   £ ☐   £ ☐

Note for parent: This activity gives practice in totalling coins and exact pounds.

Giving change

Draw coins to show the change from 20p.
Write the amount of change.

7p [ ] [ ]p

8p [ ] [ ]p

12p [ ] [ ]

15p [ ] [ ]p

Write the change from 20p for each of these.

11p change: [ ] p

14p change: [ ] p

6p change: [ ] p

9p change: [ ] p

16p change: [ ] p

Note for parent: To work out the amount of change your child needs to count on from the price up to 20p.

117

Hidden numbers

Leaves have hidden some of the numbers on the snakes. Write the missing numbers.

$8 + \square = 11$

$9 - \square = 5$

$\square - 6 = 6$

$\square + 6 = 13$

$\square + 12 = 25$

$30 - \square = 3$

$\square - 15 = 9$

$23 + \square = 53$

Work out the answers. Colour the even numbers red. Colour the odd numbers blue. Which number is hidden in the picture?

$7 - 6$	$3 + 4$	$4 + 3$	$9 - 4$
	$7 - 5$ $2 + 1$	$8 - 2$ $8 - 7$ $7 + 7$ $11 - 5$	$14 - 9$
$11 + 6$		$6 + 6$ $10 + 3$	$3 + 4$
$1 + 8$ $4 + 6$	$5 + 6$ $9 - 3$	$10 - 6$ $11 + 7$	$7 + 6$
$13 - 6$ $9 - 7$	$6 + 3$ $8 + 7$	$9 - 4$ $4 + 4$	$8 - 3$
$12 - 5$ $8 + 4$ $9 + 4$	$9 + 9$	$3 + 6$ $11 - 7$	$12 - 3$
$6 - 1$	$4 + 9$	$3 + 2$	

Note for parent: This activity gives practice in adding and taking away numbers to 20.

Quick quiz

Write the numbers to complete these adding chains.

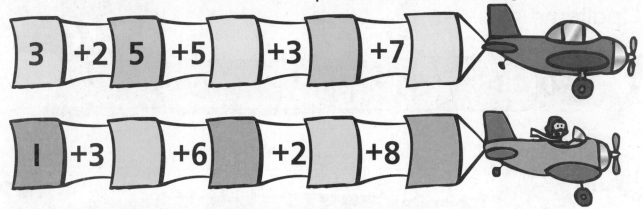

| 3 | +2 | 5 | +5 | | +3 | | +7 | |
| 1 | +3 | | +6 | | +2 | | +8 | |

Circle the odd one out in each set.

11 − 5   12 − 6

15 − 9   17 − 9

13 − 6

18 − 9

14 − 7   15 − 8

Write the change from 20p for each of these.

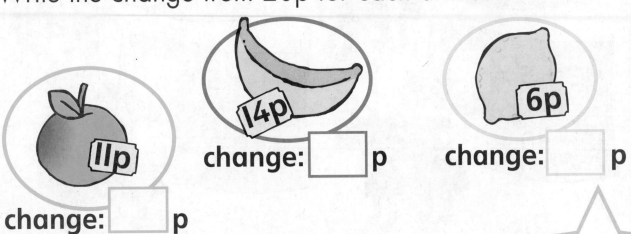

11p

change: ☐ p

14p

change: ☐ p

6p

change: ☐ p

Note for parent: This page is another chance to revise some of the learning so far.

119

Large numbers

Write the missing numbers in these patterns.

((30 (40 (((60 ((((100 (

(90)) 110) 120 ( )) 150))

Write the totals in the boxes. Use the first answer to help you to work out the second answer.

7 + 2 = ☐

70 + 20 = ☐

4 + 3 = ☐

40 + 30 = ☐

3 + 5 = ☐

30 + 50 = ☐

6 + 5 = ☐

60 + 50 = ☐

Note for parent: This activity gives practice in adding multiples of 10.

Draw a line to match each dragon to the correct cave.

120

110

90 + 60 =

70 + 70 =

50 + 80 =

90

150

50 + 70 =

140

60 + 30 =

130

70 + 40 =

Subtract large numbers

Complete these number trails.

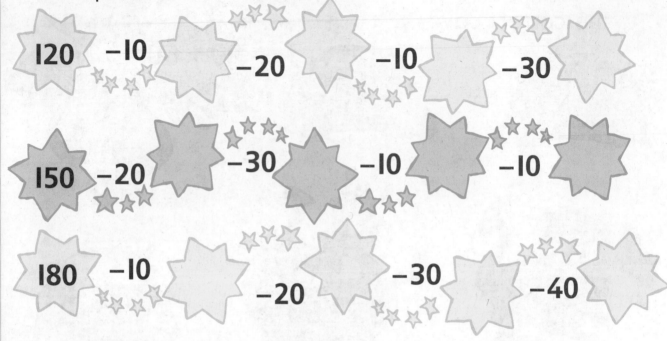

120 −10 ___ −20 ___ −10 ___ −30 ___

150 −20 ___ −30 ___ −10 ___ −10 ___

180 −10 ___ −20 ___ −30 ___ −40 ___

Answer these sums. Use the first answer to help you work out the second answer.

8 − 3 = ☐
80 − 30 = ☐

7 − 4 = ☐
70 − 40 = ☐

15 − 8 = ☐
150 − 80 = ☐

9 − 5 = ☐
90 − 50 = ☐

12 − 7 = ☐
120 − 70 = ☐

14 − 6 = ☐
140 − 60 = ☐

Note for parent: This activity gives practice in subtracting multiples of 10. Your child may need some extra support with the three-digit numbers.

Colour the flying saucers that have the same answer.
Use a different colour for each matching pair.

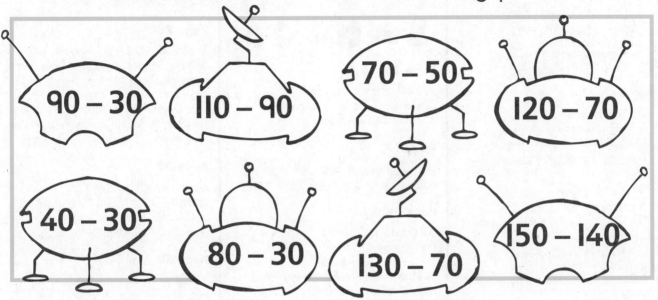

Draw lines to join the numbers with
a difference of 50.

English answers

Page 7

Page 8

1. The <u>boy</u> is reading a <u>book</u>.
2. The <u>girl</u> is watching <u>television</u>.
3. The <u>dog</u> is playing with a <u>ball</u>.
4. The <u>man</u> is cutting the <u>grass</u>.

Page 9

1. A ladybird is very <u>small</u>.
2. The leaves fell off the tree because it was <u>windy</u>.
3. The sun was shining and the sky was <u>blue</u>.
4. Dad had just picked the flowers so they were <u>fresh</u>.
5. The dog was <u>happy</u> because he had a new ball.
6. It was <u>cold</u> in the garden and there was ice on the pond.

Pages 10-11

Page 12

fly, frog, coat, apple, balloon, lamb, bread, pear, queen.

Page 13

boy – A male child.
hutch – A pet rabbit's home.
monster – A creature you read about in fairy tales.
saw – A tool that has sharp metal teeth.
penguin – A black-and-white bird that cannot fly.

Page 14

top: sleeping, licking.
middle: running, climbing.
bottom: swimming, flying.

Page 15

two – 2, six – 6, three – 3, eight – 8, ten – 10, four – 4, seven – 7, nine – 9, one – 1, five – 5.

er   ce   ake   ar   tch   ing

Page 16

1. November. 2. January.
3. October. 4. July. 5. September.
6. May and December.

Page 17

<u>l</u>eaf, sn<u>ail</u>, <u>p</u>each, <u>seal</u>, <u>pail</u>, <u>seat</u>.
<u>b</u>oat, <u>m</u>ouse, <u>c</u>oat, <u>c</u>loud, <u>r</u>oad, tr<u>ou</u>sers.

Page 18

Possible answers are:
Dad is playing with a red ball.
The baby is eating a big ice cream.
The brown dog is chasing the cat.
Mum is feeding the hungry ducks.

Page 19

starfish, waterfall, homework, playtime, toothbrush, football, earring, bookmark.

Page 20

<u>b</u>ear – <u>p</u>ear – <u>w</u>ear; <u>f</u>ire – <u>w</u>ire – <u>h</u>ire; <u>j</u>aw – <u>cl</u>aw – <u>str</u>aw; <u>br</u>own – <u>cl</u>own – <u>cr</u>own; <u>fl</u>ight – <u>br</u>ight – <u>kn</u>ight.

Page 21

1. Kelly and Sam; 2. Sam and Anna; 3. Kelly and Anna; 4. Kelly and Anna; 5. Sam and Anna; 6. Kelly and Anna.

Page 22

1. Parrot said, "I like to fly and sing." 2. Monkey said, "I love to eat bananas." 3. Horse said, "I like to eat hay." 4. Kangaroo said, "I like to jump and hop." 5. Elephant said, "I have a long trunk."

Page 23

is not – isn't; cannot – can't;
I would – I'd; I am – I'm;
will not – won't; you have – you've.

<u>I'd</u> like to see you but <u>I'm</u> ill. I <u>can't</u> go out but <u>I'd</u> like to see you if <u>you've</u> time and <u>it's</u> not too far for you to come.

Page 27

1. silly; 2. sensible; 3. silly; 4. silly; 5. silly; 6. sensible.

Page 28

1. May; 2. shape; 3. paint; 4. lion; 5. man. Shapes: square, triangle, circle, rectangle; Farm animals: sheep, horse, pig, cow; Vehicles: bus, car, lorry, van; Days of week: Monday, Friday, Tuesday, Sunday; Colours: red, orange, blue, green.

Page 29

is not – isn't; I would – I'd; cannot – can't. Nouns: dog, mouse, tree; Verbs: grows, run, squeaks; Adjectives: tall, soft, cold.

Page 30

1. wet – dry; 2. soft – hard; 3. first – last; 4. far – near; 5. empty – full; 6. hot – cold; 7. night – day; 8. push – pull; 9. short – long; 10. heavy – light.

Page 31

1. The dog barked at the burglar.
2. The horse galloped across the field.
3. The frog jumped out of the pond.
4. The birds flew into the air.
5. The spider spun a big web.
6. The cat slept on the wall.

Page 32

a	e	m	c	i	g	r	t	h	j
s	r	l	c	b	t	a	l	q	k
d	o	g	s	g	r	o	w	s	z
f	k	f	m	u	e	s	b	g	s
d	g	s	t	e	q	n	q	u	
r	u	n	s	u	f	u	d	m	p
p	x	a	l	j	y	e	u	o	n
w	f	l	o	o	v	a	l	u	t
y	a	z	e	v	n	k	y	s	b
t	h	x	a	e	c	s	w	e	d

Page 33

Some of the words you can make are: or, let, is, as, pea, at, mat, me. <u>m</u>an – <u>p</u>an; <u>c</u>oat – <u>b</u>oat; <u>robber</u> – <u>rubber</u>; <u>card</u> – <u>cart</u>; <u>fork</u> – <u>fort</u>; <u>wolf</u> – <u>golf</u>.